3 1994 00950 1278

SANTA ANA PUBLIC LIBRARY

D0633742

SANTA ANA PUBLIC LIBRARY

EXPERIMENT WITH AIR

Written by Bryan Murphy

Science Consultant: Dr. Christine Sutton
Nuclear Physics Department, University of Oxford

Education Consultant: Ruth Bessant

Lerner Publications Company
Minneapolis, Minnesota

J 533.6 MUR
Murphy, Bryan
Experiment with air

AUG 2 8 2000

CENTRAL

$19.93

31994009501278

All words marked in **bold** can be found in the glossary that begins on page 30.

This edition published in 1991 by:
Lerner Publications Company
241 First Avenue North
Minneapolis, Minnesota 55401

Text © Bryan Murphy, 1991
Compilation copyright © Two-Can Publishing Ltd, 1991

First published in 1991 by:
Two-Can Publishing Ltd.
27 Cowper Street
London EC2A 4AP

All rights reserved. International copyright secured. No part of this book may be reproduced or transmitted in any form or by any means, electronic or mechanical, including photocopying and recording, or by any information storage or retrieval system, without permission in writing from the publisher, except for the inclusion of brief quotations in an acknowledged review.

Library of Congress Cataloging-in-Publication Data

Murphy, Bryan.
   Experiment with air / written by Bryan Murphy.
      p.   cm.
   "First published in 1991 by: Two-Can Publishing Ltd. . . .
London"—T.p. verso.
   Summary: Presents simple experiments demonstrating the basic scientific principles of air.
   ISBN 0-8225-2452-X
   1. Air—Experiments—Juvenile literature. [1. Air—Experiments. 2. Experiments.] I. Title.
QC161.2.M87 1991
533'.6—dc20
                                                    91-8687
                                                    CIP
                                                    AC

Printed in Italy by Amadeus S.p.A. - Rome
Bound in the United States of America

1 2 3 4 5 6 7 8 9 10 00 99 98 97 96 95 94 93 92 91

ISBN: 0-8225-2452-X

All photographs are copyright © Fiona Pragoff, except for the following: cover, pp. 10, 14 (top), 23 (bottom center), 24 (top), 28 (bottom), ZEFA Picture Library (UK) Ltd.; pp. 8 (left and center), 9 (center left), 13 (right), 15 (bottom), 29 (bottom), NHPA; p. 8 (top right), Heather Angel/Biofotos; pp. 9 (top left), 16, 18 (top), 29 (top), Oxford Scientific Films; pp. 13 (left), 21, Quadrant Picture Library; p. 17 (top), Ann Ronan Picture Library; p. 18 (bottom), Science Photo Library.

Illustrations by Sally Kindberg.

CONTENTS

WHAT IS AIR?

Have you ever thought about **air**? You cannot see or smell it. You can only feel it when it moves quickly past you in the form of **wind**. Yet air is all around us.

Does air weigh anything? Try an experiment to find out. Blow up two balloons and hang one from each end of a strip of wood. Hang the strip of wood from the back of a chair using some string. Now you have a pair of balloon scales. With a pin, carefully make a little hole near the knot in one of the balloons to let the air out slowly. Watch what happens with your scales.

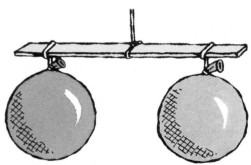

Which weighs more, an empty balloon or a balloon full of air? You can see that air weighs something. In fact, the air in a medium-sized room weighs about as much as you do.

▲ Believe it or not, you can even *pour* air. Fill a large glass tank with water. Trap some air by pushing an upside-down beaker to the bottom of the tank. Carefully pour the air into another beaker as shown. See if you can do this without spilling any air.

▲ When you **breathe** in, you take air into your lungs. How much air do you think your lungs hold? You can measure the air by blowing through a plastic tube into a measuring jug held upside down in a tank of water. You will be surprised how much air you breathe in and out.

◀ Candles need air to be able to burn. Ask an adult to light two candles for you. Put a large jar over one and a small jar over the other. Which candle goes out first?

HEAVY AIR AND LEMONADE

The **atmosphere** is a heavy layer of air around the Earth. The **pressure** of all this air pushing down on each square yard (square meter) of Earth is about the same as the **weight** of 400 children. Yet the air does not crush you because the pressure is equal on all sides. The air all around us supports the weight of the air from above.

Tell a friend you can crush a plastic bottle without touching it. Ask an adult to pour one cup of very hot tap water into the bottle. Screw the lid on tightly and shake the bottle. Wait and see what happens.

At lower temperatures air has less pressure. As the air inside the bottle cools, the pressure goes down. There is less support inside for the walls of the bottle.

▼ The outside air will crush the walls.

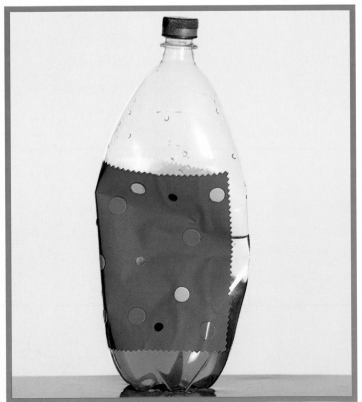

◀ Every time you drink through a straw, you suck air out of the straw and leave an empty space inside it. The heavy air from outside pushes the on liquid in your bottle and forces it up into the straw to fill the empty space.

▼ Try sealing a straw into the mouth of a bottle with modeling clay. What happens? The heavy air cannot get inside the bottle to push the liquid up into the straw, so you cannot drink.

FLYING SEEDS

When a plant makes seeds, it needs to spread them out so new young plants will grow. There are many different kinds of seeds and many ways of spreading them.

▲ Some seeds have little hooks that stick to people's clothing or cling to the fur of animals. Eventually the seeds fall off, and new plants grow.

◀ Air also scatters seeds. Some seeds are very small and can be carried far away by the wind. Can you see how?

▼ The maple tree has a seed that looks like a **propeller**. When the maple seeds fall from high branches, they spin slowly to the ground. A steady wind might carry them far away. Do you have a maple tree in your neighborhood?

▼ Make your own **helicopter** with a piece of paper. Cut out the shape below. Fold the bottom flaps toward the center and weight this end with a paper clip. Throw your helicopter into the air. What happens?

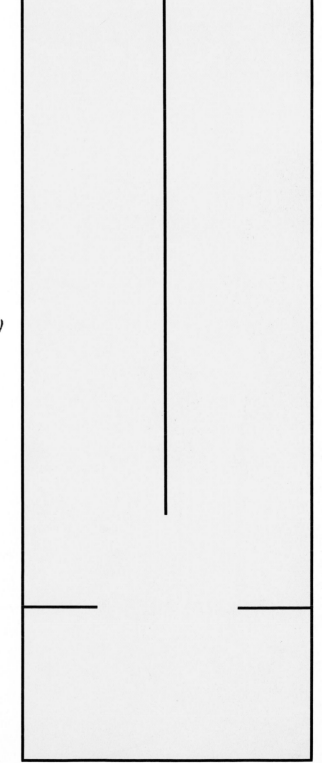

PARACHUTES

◄ When sky divers jump out of airplanes, **parachutes** slow the divers down so that they can land safely on the ground. As a parachute travels downward, air pushes up against it and prevents **gravity** from tugging the diver to the ground so quickly.

Never jump from a great height yourself. It is very dangerous.

► Sometimes airplane pilots drop large crates of supplies in rocky or hilly places where it is too difficult to land. A big parachute slows the heavy load down as it falls. But if the parachute is too big, the supplies may drift too slowly in the air and land in the wrong place.

◄ Returning from the moon, a spacecraft splashes down in the ocean. Parachutes are needed to slow its descent.

▼ You can make a parachute out of tissue paper. Put a hole in each corner.

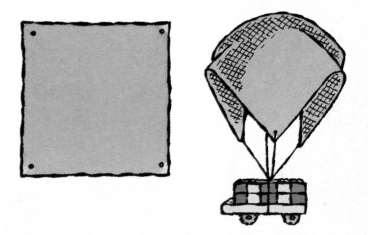

Strengthen the holes with paper reinforcers. Tie the parachute to a toy truck with thread. Drop it from a high place. If you cut a hole in the center of the parachute, what happens? Is it easier to hit the target?

FABULOUS FLYING MACHINES

Can a sheet of paper fly? Of course it can. But it must be the right shape so that it can cut through the air.

▶Start with a rectangular sheet of paper and fold it into a dart shape like this.

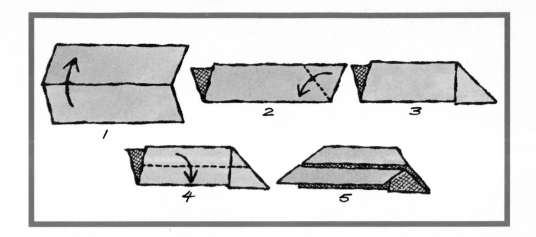

Real airplanes must be **streamlined** just like paper airplanes. But real airplanes have **engines** to push them. Air moves faster over the wings than under them because of the shape of the wings. The slow-moving air underneath pushes up on the wings, and this lifts the airplane. Birds' wings work the same way.

◀ Tape some thread to two Ping-Pong balls and hang them about two inches (five centimeters) apart from the back of a chair. Ask a friend to try to move both balls without touching them. Can you think how to do it using moving air?

All you have to do is blow between the balls and they will move together. Try it.

13

HOT AIR RISING

Warm air is lighter than cold air. Just like a bubble of air floating to the surface in water, warm air rises. Indoors, the warm air cools when it reaches the ceiling, and then it sinks down again.

You can use rising air to power a spinning snake.

▼ Trace this shape onto thin cardboard and cut it out. With a parent's help, attach a pencil to the top of a radiator or heater with a piece of modeling clay. Balance the snake on the tip of the pencil.

▶ The hot air from the heater will rise, and it will turn the snake. Color your snake to make it more life-like. You could also give it a forked tongue.

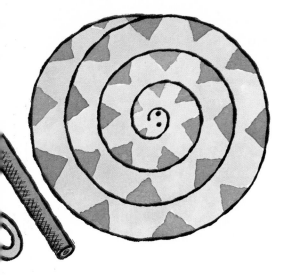

◀ Hang gliders look like big kites. They do not have engines, so they need a column of hot, rising air (called a thermal) to stay up in the sky. Do you think hang gliding would be easier on a hot day or a cold day?

Have you ever watched hang glider pilots? They must find a high hill where they can launch themselves into the air and where the warm thermals will keep them gliding for a long time. The pilot hangs from a har-ness and steers the glider with a control bar.

TRAPPING AIR TO KEEP WARM

Have you ever noticed how a pot of tea will get cold if it is left for some time? Where do you think the heat goes? It is taken away by passing air currents. Can you think how to stop the air currents?

▲ If you watch someone cooking in a kitchen, you might see **steam** rising into the air from very hot water in a saucepan. Do you think the steam could be taking some heat away with it? What do you think would happen if you put a lid on the saucepan? Would it keep the water hot longer?

◄ In some countries it is very cold, and people have to stay warm and keep heat from escaping from their bodies. They wear special clothes that trap the air next to their skin.

▲ Animals must keep warm too. These polar bears live where there is plenty of ice and snow. They grow thick fur in several layers to trap air next to their skin.

▶ Ducks spend much of their time in cold water. They have waterproof feathers on the outside to keep the water out and fluffy feathers close to their bodies to keep the warm air in. Ducks spend a lot of time taking care of their feathers to keep them in good condition.

HOT AIR BALLOONS

About two hundred years ago, the Montgolfier brothers in France noticed that hot smoke and steam move upwards. They thought that if they could trap some hot air in a large balloon, it would be able to fly.

► In September 1783, the brothers made a huge balloon out of very light material and carefully started a fire underneath it. The first passengers in the **hot air balloon** were a sheep, a chicken, and a duck. The first flight was a great success except that the sheep stepped on the chicken!

▼ Make your own hot air balloon. Ask an adult to help you cut out six shapes like this from large pieces of tissue paper. Carefully glue them together along the sides, but leave the bottom open.

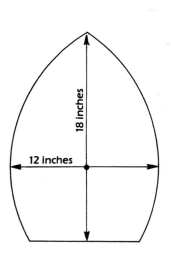

18 inches

12 inches

► Now ask an adult to fill the balloon with hot air from a hair dryer and watch what happens.

WIND POWER

When the sun shines, it heats up the land and the air above the land. The hot air rises, and cold air rushes in to take its place. We call this wind. There are many different kinds of wind, from light breezes to powerful tornadoes.

On a windy day you can see the air moving the leaves and branches on trees, and you can feel it tugging at your clothes. The wind has a lot of **energy**, and this energy can be useful.

◀ For centuries, people have used **windmills** to pump water and to grind grain. This modern power station uses hundreds of windmills to turn the wind's energy into electricity.

You can have fun using wind energy to power races with your friends. You can make land boats like these out of old toy cars, some modeling clay, straws, and thin cardboard for the sails. Experiment with sails of different sizes and shapes. Which sails make the land boats go fastest?

Use your mouth to blow on the sails. Do the boats move faster when you blow on the sails through a straw? Try using an electric fan. Which way works best?

PUTTING OUT THE LIGHT

Air is a mixture of different **gases**. One of these gases is **oxygen**. When something burns, it needs oxygen. Without enough oxygen, the fire will go out.

▼ Here is a trick that puts out a candle flame, as if by magic. You will need a deep bowl, a short candle, vinegar, and baking soda.

Put the candle in the center of the bowl and sprinkle about one tablespoon of baking soda around it. Ask an adult to light the candle.

How can you put out the candle without blowing on the flame? Simple—just pour a small amount of vinegar onto the baking soda and watch what happens.

As soon as the vinegar touches the baking soda, it foams up and gives off a gas that we cannot see. The gas is heavier than air, so instead of floating away, it slowly starts to fill the bowl. When the gas reaches the candle flame, it shuts out the oxygen and puts out the fire.

Never play with fire or matches without an adult.

The gas that you have made is called **carbon dioxide**. These firefighter trainees are learning how to use carbon dioxide foam to put out a fire.

SOUNDS FUN

When you tap an object like a drum, its surface quivers, or vibrates, and releases energy into the air. You cannot see the **vibrations**, but they travel to your ears, where you hear them as **sounds**.

▶ Make a cone from thick paper. Ask a friend to shout from the other side of the yard. Can you hear best with the narrow end or the wide end of the cone to your ear? Which gathers more sound waves?

▲ Tie a spoon to the center of a piece of string and hold the ends of the string in your ears. Have a friend tap your spoon with another spoon. Does the sound travel along the string?

▲ Make holes through the bottoms of two yogurt containers. Put a piece of string through the holes and knot the ends so they do not slip through. Have a friend hold one container and walk far enough away to pull the string tight. Put one container to your ear and ask your friend to speak into the other container. You now have a portable telephone.

◀ Hold a balloon filled with water next to your ear. Ask a friend to hold a ticking watch against the other side of the balloon. Can you still hear the ticking through the water?

▼ Strike a triangle to make a loud ringing sound. What happens if you touch the triangle while it's still ringing?

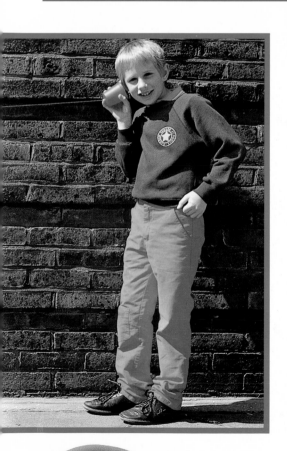

◀ Did you know that **thunder** is the sound made by **lightning**? You see lightning before you hear thunder because sound travels more slowly than light does. You can figure out how far away lightning is by counting the seconds between the lightning flash and the bang of the thunder. Divide by five to find the distance in miles or by three to find the distance in kilometers.

25

MAKING MUSIC

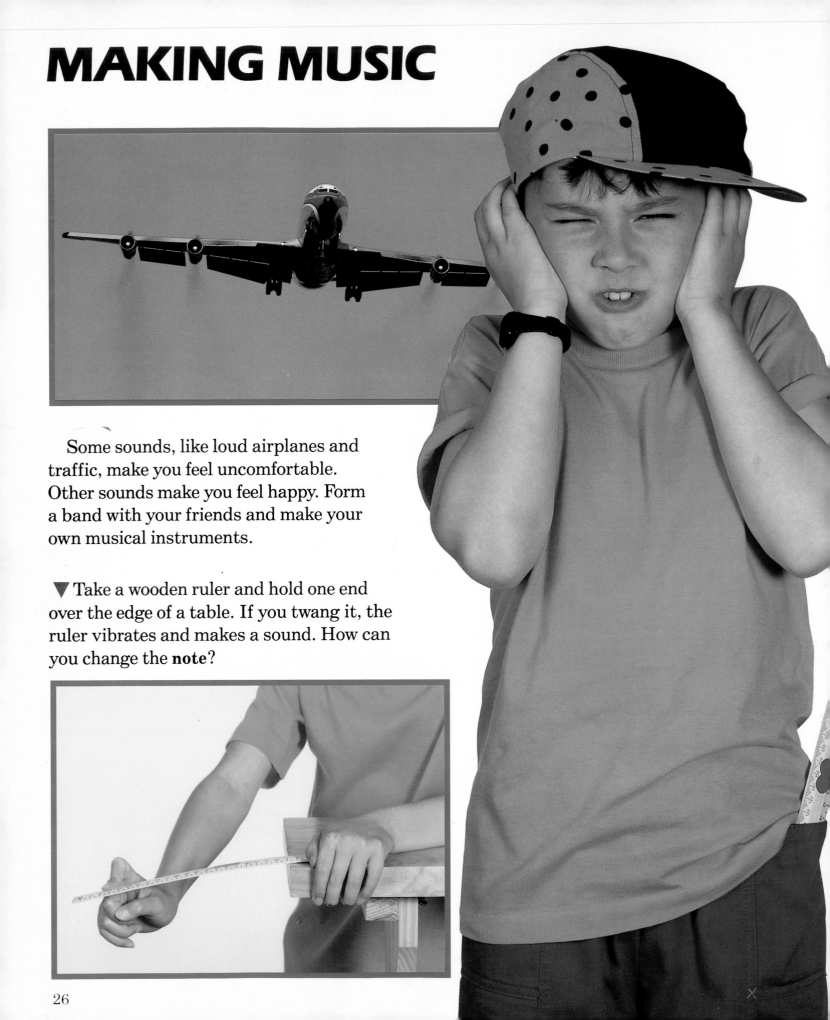

Some sounds, like loud airplanes and traffic, make you feel uncomfortable. Other sounds make you feel happy. Form a band with your friends and make your own musical instruments.

▼ Take a wooden ruler and hold one end over the edge of a table. If you twang it, the ruler vibrates and makes a sound. How can you change the **note**?

◀ Wrap some brown paper tightly over a box. When you hit the paper with a wooden stick or ruler, it sounds like a drum. Make some big drums and some little ones. Can you put them in order of high and low sounds?

▼ Use two large saucepan lids, one in each hand, to make a pair of cymbals.

▼ Make an instrument from glass bottles filled with water. If you gently tap the side of each bottle, it makes a nice sound.

You can make different notes by changing the amount of water in the bottles.

◀ You can also make an instrument with a row of glasses filled with different amounts of water. Wet your index finger and rub it quickly around the top of the glass until you hear a ringing sound. Each glass will give you a different musical note.

PANPIPES AND GUITARS

Here are some more instruments you can make.

▶ Fold some tracing paper over a comb, touch the comb gently to your lips, and hum a tune.

▼ To make a set of panpipes, ask an adult to cut some old garden hose to different lengths. Glue or tape the hose pipes together on a piece of cardboard in order of size. Close the bottom of each pipe with some thin cardboard. If you blow across the top of each pipe it makes a good whistling noise. Which pipe makes the highest note?

▼ To make your own guitar you need a long thin box. Glue a cardboard rectangle inside the box. The cardboard should be a little taller than the box itself. Stretch rubber bands of different thicknesses along the length of the box. The rubber bands should rest on the cardboard in the center. Pluck the rubber bands and they will vibrate and make a noise. Can you see what makes different notes?

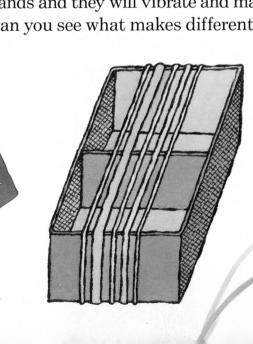

Paint all your musical instruments in different colors. Make music with your friends.

GLOSSARY

air: the mixture of oxygen and other gases that surrounds the Earth. Humans and animals breathe air.

atmosphere: another name for the layer of gas that surrounds the Earth

breathe: to take air into your lungs

carbon dioxide: a gas in the air that plants use to make food. People use carbon dioxide to put out certain fires.

energy: the power to do work

engine: a device that uses electricity or fuel to power a machine or a vehicle

gas: a substance, like oxygen, that has no definite shape. All substances are either liquid, solid, or gas.

gravity: the force that pulls things to the ground

helicopter: an aircraft with rotating blades that help it to stay up in the air

hot air balloon: a giant balloon that can carry people into the air. Hot air is lighter than cool air, so when the air inside the balloon is heated, the balloon rises.

lightning: a stroke of electricity created during some rainstorms

note: a musical sound

oxygen: a gas that humans and animals must breathe in order to live

parachute: a big sail that slows down people or objects that fall from great heights. Sky divers use parachutes when they jump from airplanes.

pressure: the force of air pushing on an object

propeller: a whirling blade that pushes an airplane or vehicle forward

sound: a vibration that we can hear

steam: small water droplets in the air

streamlined: shaped to travel smoothly through liquid or air

thunder: the sound made when a lightning stroke heats up the air

vibration: a quivering movement that sends out waves of energy

weight: the force of something pushing downward

wind: moving air

windmill: a shaft with large blades that uses wind energy to create electricity or to operate machinery

INDEX

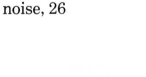